Amphibious Ships

by Michael Green

Consultant:

Jack A. Green

Naval Historical Center

CAPSTONE
HIGH/LOW BOOKS
an imprint of Capstone Press
Mankato, Minnesota

Capstone High/Low Books are published by Capstone Press
818 North Willow Street • Mankato, MN 56001
http://www.capstone-press.com

Library of Congress Cataloging-in-Publication Data
Green, Michael, 1952–
    Amphibious ships/by Michael Green.
        p. cm. — (Land and sea)
    Includes bibliographical references and index.
    Summary: Discusses the history and military uses of the ships and
related equipment used for amphibious assaults, highlighting specific
models and their roles in various battles.
    ISBN 0-7368-0040-9
    1. Amphibious assault ships—United States—Juvenile literature.
[1. Amphibious assault ships. 2. Warships.] I. Title. II. Series: Land and
sea (Mankato, Minn.)
V895.G74 1999
359.9'85'0973—dc21
                              98-15238
                                 CIP
                                 AC

Editorial Credits
Matt Doeden, editor; James Franklin, cover designer and illustrator;
  Sheri Gosewisch, photo researcher

Photo Credits
Archive Photos, 16
Department of Defense, 26
DOD — Defense Visual Information Center — March ARB California, 32
National Archives, 18
U.S. Coast Guard Public Affairs, 12
U.S. Navy, cover, 4, 6, 8, 11, 15, 21, 24, 28, 30, 35, 36, 38, 40, 47

Table of Contents

Chapter 1

Amphibious Ships

Amphibious ships carry troops and supplies across bodies of water. They can move troops and supplies from sea to land quickly. Amphibious ships allow troops to attack enemies on coastlines and islands. Some people call amphibious ships amphibs.

The navy uses amphibious ships to make amphibious assaults. Troops attack targets on land from ships during amphibious assaults. Some amphibs carry only equipment such as tanks. Other amphibs carry people. Crews on amphibious ships must bring troops and their

Amphibious ships carry troops and supplies across bodies of water.

Amphibious ships come in many sizes.

equipment to shore safely. They must be
prepared to pick up troops when battles
are finished.

Size and Speed

Amphibious ships are a variety of sizes.
People use displacement to measure the sizes

of ships. A ship pushes water away from itself while it is afloat. Displacement is the weight of that water. The largest amphibious ships have displacements of about 40,000 tons (about 36,000 metric tons). The smallest amphibious ships have displacements of six tons (5.4 metric tons).

Most amphibious ships are slow. People measure the speeds of ships and boats in knots. One knot equals 1.15 miles (1.85 kilometers) per hour. The fastest amphibious ships can reach speeds of 40 knots. This is about 46 miles (74 kilometers) per hour. But most travel at about 20 knots. This is about 23 miles (37 kilometers) per hour.

Tasks

The main task for amphibious ships is to transport troops and supplies from place to place. The military often needs large numbers of troops at a certain place during wartime. It needs amphibious ships to transport these troops from sea to shore.

Large amphibious ships carry troops and supplies to a landing site.

Large amphibious ships carry troops and equipment to a landing site. Few of these ships actually go onto shore. Instead, they carry some small amphibs. Crews aboard the large

amphibious ships load troops and supplies
onto the small amphibs. The small amphibs go
to shore. Crews beach the small amphibs onto
shore to deliver their troops and supplies.

Weapons and Escorts

Amphibious ships are not fighting ships. They carry few weapons. Most amphibious ships have some guns. Crew members aboard amphibious ships use guns only when enemies attack them. Crew members try to avoid enemy warships. Sometimes they use smoke to hide from enemies.

Large amphibious ships may carry some missiles and torpedoes. A missile is an explosive that can fly long distances. A torpedo is an explosive that travels underwater.

Large warships such as destroyers serve as escorts for amphibious ships. An escort is a warship that travels with and protects another ship. Escorts protect amphibious ships from enemy fleets. A fleet is a group of warships under one command.

Large warships such as destroyers serve as escorts for amphibious ships.

Chapter 2

World War II

The U.S. Navy did not need amphibious
ships until World War II (1939–1945). Troops
fought much of World War II on small islands
in the Pacific Ocean. U.S. military leaders
needed ships that could easily carry troops and
supplies to land.

The navy began building two main groups
of amphibious ships in 1940. One group was
small amphibious ships. These ships could
carry troops and supplies directly onto land.
The navy called these ships landing craft.

The other group was large amphibious
ships. Most large amphibious ships stayed in

**The U.S. Navy built small amphibious ships to carry
troops and supplies directly onto land.**

the water at all times. They carried supplies, troops, and landing craft. Some large amphibs had cranes to lift supplies onto landing craft.

Landing Craft

One kind of small amphibious ship was the Landing Ship, Tank (LST). The navy used the LST to carry tanks and other large supplies to shore. LSTs could carry as many as 20 tanks.

LST crews beached their ships to deliver supplies. Crew members opened a set of doors once a ship was near shore. They extended a long ramp from inside the ship. Army or Marine Corps members drove tanks down this ramp onto shore.

Another small amphibious ship was the Landing Ship, Medium (LSM). The LSM could carry five tanks. Crews beached LSMs the same way they beached LSTs. On small shores, crews could beach the smaller LSMs more easily than the large LSTs.

Crew members aboard LSTs opened doors once the ships were near shore.

The navy used the LCI to carry troops to shore.

The navy used the Landing Craft, Infantry (LCI) to carry troops to shore. LCIs could carry as many as 188 troops.

The smallest amphibious ships were the Landing Craft, Vehicle, Personnel (LCVP). These small amphibs could carry 36 people.

LCVPs were among the most maneuverable landing craft of World War II. Maneuverable means able to move easily. Crews could beach LCVPs on small shores.

Large Amphibious Ships

The navy used large amphibious ships to transport cargo. Cargo included weapons, vehicles, and supplies. One kind of large amphibious ship was the attack cargo ship. These ships could carry more than 5,000 tons (4,536 metric tons) of cargo or up to 300 military vehicles.

The navy loaded important vehicles and weapons last on attack cargo ships. This way, troops received the weapons and armor that they needed most right away.

The attack transport was another kind of large amphibious ship of World War II. Attack transports were the same size as attack cargo ships. But attack transports carried troops instead of cargo. Each ship could carry 871 troops and their equipment.

The U.S. Navy added docks to one end of its LSDs.

During World War II, the navy built a new kind of amphibious ship called the Landing Ship, Dock (LSD). The navy added docks to one end of the LSDs. LSDs did not need large cranes to unload supplies.

Crew members loaded small landing craft on the LSDs' docks. They then lowered the docks beneath the surface of the water. The landing craft went into the water when the docks submerged. They were then able to carry troops and supplies to shore.

Amphibious Command Ships

Another kind of large amphibious ship was the command ship. Amphibious command ships carried officers instead of troops. They also carried radios, radar, and other devices to help officers track battle conditions.

The officers on command ships managed amphibious assaults. The ships usually stayed away from land. They were safer at sea. Officers used radios to give orders to crew members on each ship. Officers also managed aircraft and warships. They watched radar for enemy ships and aircraft.

War's End

In 1945, the U.S. military was planning an amphibious assault on Japan. The assault would have been the biggest amphibious assault ever. The navy prepared hundreds of large amphibious ships to carry troops and supplies. Many navy leaders believed this was

Troops received orders from officers aboard amphibious command ships.

the only way to end World War II. The leaders also knew the assault would be dangerous for U.S. troops.

The U.S. military dropped two atomic bombs on Japan in August 1945. The bombs destroyed the Japanese cities of Hiroshima and Nagasaki. The Japanese military surrendered shortly after the U.S. military dropped the bombs. World War II ended with the Japanese surrender. The U.S. military did not have to stage its amphibious assault on Japan.

Many Japanese people died when the atomic bombs exploded. But some experts believe many more people would have died if the war had continued. The amphibious assault on Japan may have taken a long time. World War II may have lasted much longer.

World War II Naval Battles of the Pacific Ocean

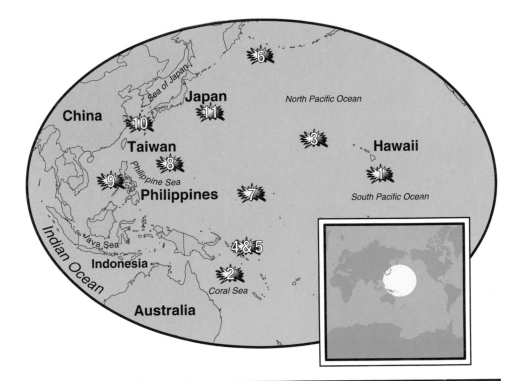

1. Pearl Harbor,
    Dec. 7, 1941
2. Battle of the Coral Sea,
    May 4-8, 1942
3. Battle of Midway,
    June 3-6, 1942
4. Guadalcanal Campaign,
    Aug. 1942 to Feb. 1943
5. Northern Solomons Campaign,
    Feb. 22, 1943 to Nov. 21, 1944
6. Battle of the Komandorski Islands,
    Mar. 26, 1943

7. Truk Attack,
    Feb. 17-18, 1944
8. Battle of the Philippine Sea,
    June 19-20, 1944
9. Leyte Campaign,
    Oct. 17, 1944 to July 1, 1945
10. Sinking of the *Yamato,*
    Apr. 7, 1945
11. Destruction of the Japanese navy,
    July 10 to Aug. 15, 1945

Chapter 3

Recent History

Some U.S. leaders felt amphibious ships were no longer useful after World War II. They believed the landing craft were too slow. The navy scrapped many of its small amphibious ships. The navy needed other ways to bring troops and supplies to shore. Navy leaders chose helicopters to replace the small amphibs.

Helicopters

Large amphibious ships began carrying helicopters during the 1950s. Helicopters could take off and land almost anywhere. They did not need large landing strips like other aircraft needed. Helicopters took over many of the

After World War II, navy leaders chose helicopters to replace small amphibious ships.

roles small amphibious ships held during
World War II.

Helicopters were better than landing craft
under most conditions. Landing craft were
slow. Enemies could see where landing craft
would reach shore. Enemies could not know
where helicopters would land. Pilots could
land helicopters in places that were safer from
enemy attacks. Helicopters were fast too.
Enemies could not react to them as quickly.

Helicopter Carriers

The navy's large amphibious ships could not
carry many helicopters. So the navy built a
new kind of amphibious ship. It was the
helicopter carrier.

The first class of helicopter carriers entered
naval service in 1961. The navy built seven
Iwo Jima class helicopter carriers. These ships
were 556 feet (169 meters) long. They had
crews of 700 people. They could transport

The navy built helicopter carriers to carry helicopters.

Each Iwo Jima class carrier had about 25 helicopters.

2,000 troops. Each carrier had about 25 helicopters to move troops and supplies to shore.

The navy had problems with its Iwo Jima class carriers. Helicopters did not operate well in bad weather. Small amphibs like those used during World War II did work well in bad

weather. The navy needed small amphibs to carry troops and supplies when helicopters could not fly. Iwo Jima carriers did not have room for these ships.

The navy built a new class of helicopter carrier. It was the Tarawa class. Tarawa class

carriers have room for small amphibs. They also can carry more than 30 helicopters or Harrier aircraft. Harrier aircraft can take off like helicopters.

The navy built five Tarawa class carriers. The ships were 833 feet (254 meters) long. They had crews of about 900 people and could carry almost 2,000 troops.

LSTs

The navy built two new classes of Landing Ship, Tanks (LSTs) after World War II. The first class was the Suffolk County class. The navy built three LSTs in this class.

The navy began building Newport class LSTs in the 1960s. The navy built 20 of these ships. During the late 1990s, two Newport class LSTs were still in service.

The navy continued to build LSTs after World War II.

Chapter 4

Today and the Future

The navy has few amphibious ships today. About 36 large amphibious ships and about 700 small amphibs are still in service. These ships are faster than the amphibs of the past. Some can reach speeds of 40 knots. Modern amphibs also carry more powerful weapons.

Wasp Class Carriers

The U.S. Navy's first Wasp class carrier entered service in 1989. Wasp class carriers are the largest class of amphibious ships the navy has ever built. They are 844 feet

Wasp class carriers are the largest amphibious ships the navy has ever built.

(257 meters) long. They have displacements of more than 40,000 tons (more than 36,000 metric tons). Each carrier has a crew of more than 1,000 people and can carry 1,875 troops.

Wasp class carriers can carry 42 transport helicopters or Harrier aircraft. They also carry small amphibs. Wasp class carriers have hospitals on board. The hospitals can house as many as 600 wounded troops.

Aircraft

The navy uses two kinds of helicopters on amphibious ships. They are the Sea Knight and the Sea Stallion. The Sea Knight can carry 25 troops. It has a rear ramp for unloading cargo. The Sea Knight's top speed is 161 miles (259 kilometers) per hour. The Sea Stallion is the navy's largest helicopter. It can carry 38 troops. Its top speed is 196 miles (315 kilometers) per hour.

Helicopters are not as fast as airplanes. Enemies can shoot down helicopters easily.

The Sea Knight can carry 25 troops.

The navy is building a new kind of airplane
called the V-22 Osprey. The Osprey will
combine features of airplanes and helicopters.
It will perform many of the same tasks as
helicopters. The aircraft will have the speed of

an airplane. Navy leaders hope to have the Osprey in service by 2001.

The Osprey will have special rotors to lift it off the ground. It will be able to tilt its rotors toward the ground like a helicopter. The Osprey's tilting rotors will allow it to take off and land like a helicopter.

Landing Craft, Air Cushioned

Navy leaders saw a need for a faster landing craft to use on its Landing Ship, Docks (LSDs). The navy built the Landing Craft, Air Cushioned (LCAC) in the early 1980s.

The LCAC is a hovercraft. It travels over water on jets of air. LCACs can reach many areas of shore other landing craft cannot. The air beneath the LCACs protect them from rough coastlines that might damage other craft.

The LCAC is 87 feet (27 meters) long. It weighs about 102 tons (93 metric tons). It has

The LCAC is a hovercraft.

The LCAC can carry 24 troops.

a crew of five people and can carry 24 troops. It can reach speeds up to 40 knots when fully loaded. The LCAC uses two large propellers to give it this speed. These blades push the LCAC through the water.

LPD-17

The U.S. Navy is building a new kind of amphibious ship called the Landing Personnel Dock-17 (LPD-17). The LPD-17 will be able to transport both troops and cargo. It also will have a dock like a Landing Ship, Dock (LSD).

The LPD-17 will carry 720 troops and their equipment. It will have both landing craft and helicopters to transport troops.

The LPD-17 will be heavily armed. It will carry powerful guns and missiles. The LPD-17 will have armor to protect it from enemy fire.

Many navy leaders believe there is little chance for major wars today. But the navy builds ships like the LPD-17 to stay prepared for possible future wars.

Wasp class carrier

Sea Knight Helicopters

Flight Deck

Masts

Smoke Stack

Elevator

Hull

Words to Know

amphibious (am-FIB-ee-uhss)—able to work on land or water

armor (AR-mur)—a protective metal covering

assault (uh-SAWLT)—an attack

beach (BEECH)—to move onto shore

cargo (KAR-goh)—the goods carried by a ship or aircraft

displacement (diss-PLAYSS-muhnt)—the weight of the water a ship pushes away from itself while afloat

escort (ESS-kort)—a warship that travels with and protects another ship

fleet (FLEET)—a group of warships under one command

hovercraft (HUHV-ur-kraft)—a vehicle that can travel over land and water on jets of air

knot (NOT)—a measurement of speed for ships; one knot equals 1.15 miles per hour.

maneuverable (muh-NOO-ver-uh-buhl)—able to move easily

missile (MISS-uhl)—an explosive that can fly long distances

propeller (pruh-PEL-ur)—a set of rotating blades that pushes a craft through air or water

radar (RAY-dar)—machinery that uses radio waves to locate or guide objects

rotor (ROH-tur)—a set of rotating blades that lifts an aircraft off the ground

submerge (suhb-MURJ)—to push below the surface of the water

surrender (suh-REN-dur)—to give up a fight or battle

torpedo (tor-PEE-doh)—an explosive that travels underwater

transport (transs-PORT)—to move something from one place to another

To Learn More

Green, Michael. *Amphibious Vehicles.* Land and Sea. Mankato, Minn.: Capstone Press, 1997.

Green, Michael. *The United States Marine Corps.* Serving Your Country. Mankato, Minn.: Capstone High/Low Books, 1998.

Green, Michael. *The United States Navy.* Serving Your Country. Mankato, Minn.: Capstone High/Low Books, 1998.

Naden, Corinne J. and Rose Blue. *The U.S. Navy.* Defending Our Country. Brookfield, Conn.: Millbrook Press, 1993.

Useful Addresses

Bonhomme Richard (Wasp class carrier)
Commanding Officer
PCD Bonhomme Richard (LHD 6)
3975 Norman Scott Road, Suite 1 N3
San Diego, CA 92136-5588

Naval Historical Center
Washington Navy Yard
901 M Street SE
Washington, DC 20374-5060

Navy Public Affairs Office
Naval Sea Systems Command
Washington, DC 20362

Internet Sites

Naval Historical Center
http://www.history.navy.mil/

Navy Fact File: Amphibious Assault Ships
http://www.defenselink.mil/factfile

U.S. Navy: Welcome Aboard
http://www.navy.mil

USS Wasp
http://www.spear.navy.mil/ships/lhd1/docs/
  go.html

Index